not my kid

A No-BS Guide to Stopping Predators

s. t. ashman

ashman books

contents

1. Please Help Them! — 1
2. Who I Am—And Why I'm Writing This — 3
3. This Isn't About Paranoia. It's About Smart Parenting. — 5
4. What This Guide Is (and Isn't) — 6
5. Section 1: Who Are the Predators? (And Where Are They?) — 9
6. How Grooming Works — 12
7. Section 2: The Body Safety Rules Every Kid Needs to Know — 14
8. Safe vs. Unsafe Touch—No Exceptions — 21
9. "Your Body, Your Rules"—They Don't Owe Affection to Anyone — 25
10. The "NO Game" (How to Practice Saying No) — 27
11. Code Words, Exit Strategies, and the "What If" Game — 29
12. The "What If" Game — 31
13. Section 3: The Places We Overlook (And How to Fix It) — 32
14. Overtrusting People You Think Are Safe — 35
15. Sleepovers—How to Rethink Them — 37
16. One-on-One Time—Like Tutoring or Lessons — 39
17. Tech Is a Gateway — 40
18. What You Can Do Differently Today — 42
19. Section 4: Safety Drills and Real-Life Conversations — 43
20. Secrecy Is Their Biggest Weapon — 44
21. How to Practice Situations Like Fire Drills — 45
22. Repetition Builds Confidence — 48
23. Create a Shame-Free Zone — 49
24. Section 5: If Something Happens—What Now? — 50
25. Signs of Abuse Most Parents Miss — 51
26. If Your Child Discloses—What to Say, What Not to Say — 52
27. When You Suspect Something But Don't Have Proof — 54

28. Who to Call, How to Report, and Where to Find Support — 55
29. Get Professional Help Right Away — 56
30. Final Chapter: No More Easy Targets — 58
31. Your Parent Checklist — 59
32. Reminder: You Won't Do This Perfectly—And That's Okay — 61
33. A Few Final Words of Encouragement — 62
34. Before You Close This Book—Please Remember — 63
35. Thank you! — 64

About the Author — 67

Copyright © 2025 S. T. ASHMAN

All rights reserved.

please help them!

. . .

<u>"I DON'T NEED to be violent," he said, his tone flat, like he was going through a grocery list. "Especially not with the small ones. I just make them feel like they're bad. Like it's all their fault."</u>
—H. S., predator, during a therapy session

<u>*Please Help Them!*</u>
Dear Readers,
Please consider leaving a review on Amazon, Goodreads, or any place where books are shared. Your words matter more than you know. Your review could be the reason someone picks up *Not My Kid!* Your voice could truly save a life.

Dear Influencers,
You have a platform, and people listen when you speak. Even a short post or quick mention of this book can spread awareness. I'm asking—heart to heart—please lend me your voice, just for a moment, for the sake of our children.

. . .

S. T. Ashman

Dear Booksellers,

This book is available at a discount through IngramSpark. You won't make a huge profit. You'll likely just break even after shipping. But you'll be doing something deeply meaningful—helping protect children. Your customers will remember and respect your store for that choice. And for transparency: I don't make money on this book either. This isn't about sales. It's about something too important to ignore.

Dear Teachers, Therapists, Doctors, and Other Professionals,

Please email me at **hello@ashmanbooks.com**. I can offer discounted copies for about $2.50/book—and I'll cover the shipping. Whatever it takes to get this book into the hands of those who need it.

From the bottom of my heart—thank you for making a difference.

who i am—and why i'm writing this
. . .

I'm a former licensed psychotherapist.

I SPENT years working in correctional facilities, inpatient psych units, and outpatient clinics. I've worked with survivors of sexual abuse—children and adults. And I've worked with the people who hurt them—pedophiles, rapists, and children who went on to harm others because someone harmed them first.

The pattern is clear.

Predators rarely carry the blame or show remorse.

Survivors carry the pain for life. They experience shame, confusion, fear, self-blame, nightmares, panic attacks, and depression.

They wonder what they did wrong, why no one believed them, why no one protected them.

They spend years trying to feel normal again.

Meanwhile, the predators?

Many lie. Many minimize. Many take no responsibility. Even when convicted, even on parole, even when the evidence is undeniable.

As a therapist, I've talked to them. Analyzed them. Built strategies to fight them.

Today, I'm a thriller author.

For my last book, I was working on a scene involving a child being sexually abused.

And I couldn't write it.

I tried. I deleted it. Tried again. I felt sick. Nauseous. It wasn't some dark, twisted invention—it was reality. Something that has happened millions of times in real life.

In the end, I barely mentioned the sexual abuse in the book.

I couldn't bring myself to write it.

But I couldn't let it go either. So, I decided to write this.

A short, accessible guide for parents.

FREE as an ebook. And sold only at the cost of printing and shipping for the paperback—no royalties, no profits. Because I want it in as many hands as possible.

If it helps protect even one child, it's worth it. You can't put a price tag on a child's safety. Not in my eyes.

I'm not writing this from a pedestal. I'm not promising that if you follow every step, nothing bad will ever happen.

I wish I could.

But I can't.

This guide is not a guarantee. It's an effort.

An effort to educate, equip, and help parents do everything they can to protect their children.

And if something *has* happened—or ever does—there's a section at the end of this book on what to do, where to turn, and how to get help *immediately*.

Even in the darkest moments, you are not alone. Your child is not broken beyond repair. And neither are you.

this isn't about paranoia. it's about smart parenting.
. . .

I'M NOT HERE to scare you. I'm not here to make you bubble-wrap your child and never let them out of your sight. That's not what this guide is about.

This guide is about prevention—real, practical, clear-eyed parenting.

It's about making your child a harder target.

It's about giving you the tools to start the right conversations early, to spot red flags, and to build the kind of safety net that predators *don't* want to tangle with.

What This Guide Is (and Isn't):
This is not a deep academic dive.
This isn't written in clinical language.
You don't need a degree or spare hours to get through it.
This is a short, to-the-point guide packed with the conversations, boundaries, and habits that could save your child.

Because no one thinks it will happen to *their* kid—until it does.

So let's make sure it doesn't.

what this guide is (and isn't)

. . .

LET'S *start with the hard truth:*

Child abuse statistics before the age of 18:

- 1 out of every 4 girls is sexually abused.
- 1 out of every 6 boys is sexually abused.
- 1 in 5 children are solicited sexually while on the internet.
- Nearly 70% of all reported sexual assaults (including assaults on adults) occur to children ages 17 and under.
- The median age for reported child abuse is 9 years old.
- 85% of child abuse victims never report their abuse.
- Nearly 50% of all victims of forcible sodomy, sexual assault with an object, and forcible fondling are children under 12.
- Over 90% of abusers are people whom children know, love, and trust.
- 30-40% of victims are abused by a family member.

- 50% are abused by someone outside of the family whom they know and trust.
- Evidence that a child has been sexually abused is not always obvious, and many children do not report that they have been abused.
- Young victims might not recognize their victimization as sexual abuse.
- Nearly 70% of child sex offenders have between 1 and 9 victims; at least 20% have 10 to 40 victims.
- An average serial child molester might have as many as 400 victims in his lifetime.
- Nearly 50% of women in prison state they were abused as children.
- Over 75% of serial rapists report they were sexually abused as youngsters.
- The way a victim's family responds to abuse plays an important role in how the incident affects the victim.
- Sexually abused children who keep it a secret or who "tell" and are not believed are at greater risk than the general population for psychological, emotional, social, and physical problems often lasting into adulthood.
- Women who report childhood rape are 3 times more likely to become pregnant before age 18.
- An estimated 60% of teen first pregnancies are preceded by experiences of molestation, rape, or attempted rape. The average age of the offender is 27 years.
- Victims of child sexual abuse are more likely to be sexually promiscuous.
- Over 75% of teenage prostitutes have been sexually abused.
- An estimated 42 million survivors of childhood sexual abuse exist in America today.

Source: https://www.d2l.org

Let that sink in.

One in four girls and one in six boys in the United States will be sexually abused before they turn 18.

Go to a birthday party.

Stand on a school playground.

Sit on a park bench and count the children running around.

▶ **<u>Every fourth girl. Every sixth boy. Some have already been abused. Others will be.</u>**

That's reality. And those are just the *reported* cases.

We live in a system that protects predators more than children. A system that makes it easy for offenders to blend in, stay hidden, and get away with it.

That's not by accident—it's the result of centuries of living under a structure in which the people writing the laws are often the very ones who benefit from keeping victims silent.

Research consistently indicates that the majority of sexual offenses are committed by males, but female perpetrators, while less common, still represent a portion of cases.

The truth is: There are people who want to harm our children, and it's our job to stay aware of that.

section 1: who are the predators? (and where are they?)

. . .

WHEN WE THINK of child predators, most of us probably picture a shadowy stranger in a van, lurking near playgrounds or offering candy. That image is comforting in a twisted way—it makes us feel like the danger is obvious. Easy to spot. Easy to avoid.

But here's the truth: Over 90% of child sexual abuse is committed by someone the child knows.

It's not the stranger in the shadows. It's the people we let into our homes. It's the family member who always shows up to help. The friend of a friend. The coach who volunteers. The tutor. The neighbor. The cousin. Sometimes, it's a sibling. Sometimes, it's a (grand)parent.

▶ <u>**Not "Stranger Danger"—It's the People We Know**</u>

In my career as a therapist, I worked with children who had been abused—and children who had abused others. I also worked with adult survivors and the perpetrators themselves. You start to notice patterns.

One of the cases that has stayed with me for years involved a ten-year-old boy. He was referred to therapy after sexually "playing" with his three-year-old stepsister. Understandably, the mother was terrified.

Eventually, the boy disclosed something heartbreaking: His stepfather had been molesting him.

The abuse didn't stop with one child—it echoed into another. That little boy didn't understand what had happened to him. He acted it out the only way he knew how. That's what abuse does—it spreads like rot. And this rot started in the most trusted circle of all: family.

Abuse Doesn't Need a Dark Alley

It can happen in:

- Homes (your home, their home, Grandma's house)
- Schools
- Churches
- Summer camps and sports teams
- Anywhere kids are entrusted to adults
- Online—from any device in your house

A close friend of mine was abused when she was 10 years old—by her 19-year-old cousin. It happened on a family vacation. In the middle of the night, while the others were asleep, he crawled into her bed and assaulted her. Nobody knew. Nobody suspected.

To the family, he was the *sweet* kid. The *helpful* cousin. The one who always wanted to play with the girls. It's chilling, isn't it?

That's how predators operate. They charm the adults and get close to the kids. And sometimes, no one finds out until decades later—if at all.

Another case close to me involved someone in my own extended family.

A child was assaulted at a friend's sleepover. But it wasn't the friend—it was the older sibling's teenage friend, also staying the night. At some point, he entered the room and assaulted my family member while everyone else was asleep.

This is what I mean when I say it's not about strangers. It's not even always about the adults you know. Sometimes, it's the other people in the house who you didn't even think about. The ones no one screens or supervises.

how grooming works
• • •

PREDATORS RARELY BEGIN WITH ABUSE. First, they build trust, until their victim lets their guard down.

▶ This process is called grooming, and it's slow, calculated, and terrifyingly effective. It looks like this:

1. Building a bond with the child—and often the family.
2. Offering gifts, special attention, or "secrets."
3. Gradually pushing physical boundaries under the guise of play or affection.
4. Isolating the child emotionally or physically.
5. Using guilt, fear, or threats to keep the child silent.

Not all grooming is the same. Some predators are repeat offenders who plan everything—every word, every move. Others act on impulse—like older kids or teens who act on their desires in the moment without a long-term plan.

Both are dangerous. Both cause lifelong harm.

And both are preventable—if we know what to look for.

What Parents Need to Know

- Predators are rarely strangers.
- They're often people we like, love, and trust.
- They groom us, too—not just our kids.
- They hide in plain sight.

We can't rely on "gut feelings" or "vibes."

▶ Many offenders are well-liked. They're the "fun uncle/aunt." The "cool coach." The "great neighbor." That's part of their strategy.

And if something feels "off," don't ignore it.

Don't tell yourself you're overreacting.

Because your kid's safety is worth a little awkwardness or suspicion.

There are good people in this world. Good families. Good men and women.

<u>But we have to stop pretending that child sexual abuse is rare.</u>

It's not. And it's not always violent or obvious. It's subtle.

It's hidden in routines. In relationships. In plain sight.

And until we name it, we can't fight it.

section 2: the body safety rules every kid needs to know

. . .

▶ **USE CORRECT ANATOMICAL TERMS—NO Nicknames**

Let's talk about one of the easiest things you can do to protect your child from sexual abuse:

Call body parts by their correct names.

Penis. Vagina. Buttocks. Chest. Breasts.

That's it. No shame, no giggles. Just facts.

We teach kids the words for "eyes," "knees," and "toes"—but when it comes to what's under their underwear, we go silent or start using nicknames like "pee-pee," "cookie," or "down there."

Here's the problem with that:

🧩 Nicknames Create Confusion

If your child tells a teacher, "He wants my cookie," that might not sound like abuse. It might not even be taken seriously. But if your child says, "He touched my vagina," there's no room for misunderstanding. That statement demands attention.

If a predator tries to use cute names to downplay what they're doing, your child will know the real words—and that it's not okay.

But when kids don't have the right words, they struggle to explain what happened. And that silence? That confusion? Predators count on it.

▶ It Teaches Body Awareness and Ownership
Using real terms helps kids:

- Understand their bodies better
- Know what's okay and what's not
- Feel confident reporting something wrong

It also sends a powerful message:
"Your body isn't shameful. You can talk to me about anything."

▶ Predators Rely on Secrecy and Shame

If a child thinks they'll get in trouble for using a word like "penis" or "vagina," they might never say anything at all. That gives abusers exactly what they want: silence.

This isn't about making kids grow up too fast—it's about giving them language that protects them.

Tips for Parents:
If you're in a home where using anatomical terms like "penis" or "vagina" feels uncomfortable or isn't allowed, you can still teach body safety clearly. But avoid words like "cookie" etc.

Say something like:

"Some people use words like penis or vagina. In our house, we use the word 'privates,' and that means the parts of your body under your underwear. Those are your private parts, and no one should touch them except to help you stay clean or healthy—and only when mom or dad are okay with it."

The goal isn't perfection. The goal is clarity—so your child understands their body, their rights, and how to speak up if something's wrong.

If you're using "privates":
"Your privates are the parts of your body covered by your underwear—like your bottom and the area where you pee. Those parts are private, which means they're just for you. No one should touch them—unless Mommy or Daddy says it's okay. No exceptions."

If you're using "penis" (for boys):
"Your penis is the part of your body you use to pee. It's a private part, and no one should touch it—unless someone like Mommy or Daddy says it's okay. No exceptions."

If you're using "vagina" (for girls):
"Your vagina is the part of your body between your legs, and it's where you pee from. It's a private part that's just for you. No one should touch it—unless someone like Mommy or Daddy says it's okay. No exceptions."

Explaining "Private" to a Child:
"Private means something that belongs just to you. Like

your thoughts or the parts of your body under your underwear. You get to decide who talks about or sees your private parts. They're not for sharing."

💬 Explaining "No Exceptions" to a Child:
"No exceptions means no one is allowed to break the rule.

Not even if they're really nice.

Not even if they say it's a secret.

Not even if they say they're helping.

The answer is *always* no—unless Mommy or Daddy say it's okay. Like when we go to the doctor, or when Mommy or Daddy need to clean you or help with a diaper rash.

But no one should *ever* play with your vagina (or penis).

Not even Mommy or Daddy. That's *never* okay. No exceptions.

And if you're ever unsure—even just a little bit—tell me right away.

You will never, ever be in trouble for telling me."

▶ Parent Note

Predators often pretend to be helpful or even act like they're doing something "normal" or "medical." Some might even *be* in trusted roles—like teachers, coaches, or healthcare providers. That's why this rule needs to be firm:

"No one is allowed to touch your penis/vagina/privates—not even someone who says they're helping. We have to ask Mommy or Daddy."

No ethical doctor will ever examine a child's genitals alone or without clear parental consent. And no "good person" will ever ask a child to keep a secret about their body.

▶ Sometimes, tragically, a parent can be the one causing

harm. When this book says "unless Mommy or Daddy say it's okay," we're assuming the parent reading it is the safe one—someone trying to prevent abuse.

The goal is to create an open, safe space where kids feel comfortable talking about their bodies. If abuse were to happen, even by a parent, open dialogue can help a child speak up—so the other parent or a trusted adult can protect them.

We walk a fine line. Kids need to trust someone. If we teach them to fear everyone, even basic care like diaper changes or applying cream can become confusing. But if we teach what's okay and what's not, they'll recognize abuse—even from someone close.

So when we say "unless Mommy or Daddy say it's okay," we mean for things like medical care or hygiene—nothing else.

Make this very clear to your child.

💬 What a Conversation with Your Child Might Look Like:

Parent:

Hey, let's talk about something really important—our bodies.

Did you know every part of your body has a name? Like your arms, your nose, your toes…and even the parts under your underwear.

Those parts have names, too—just like everything else.

Child:

They do? *(Or maybe just nods—what matters is that they're listening.)*

Parent:

Yep! Boys have a penis, and girls have a vagina. That's just what they're called.

We use the real names so that if anything ever feels weird or wrong, you can tell me exactly what happened.

(Point to the area on your own body—over your clothes—and gently invite your child to point to the same area on their own body, also over clothes. This helps them learn body awareness without embarrassment or confusion. If it feels more natural, you can have this conversation during bath time or in the shower when your child is already naked and curious about their body. Just stay calm, clear, and matter-of-fact—no shame, no awkwardness.)

Child:

But I thought it was called a pee-pee or cookie?

Parent:

Good question! Some people do call it that. Some say "pee-pee" or "cookie" or "down there." But those are just nicknames—kind of like how people say "tummy" instead of "stomach" or "Santa" instead of "Santa Claus."

Nicknames are okay to hear, but I want you to know the real names—penis and vagina—because it helps keep you safe.

Child:

Why?

Parent:

Because if you ever need to tell me or a teacher something about your body, we want them to understand exactly what you mean. Saying "my penis hurts" is a lot clearer than "my cookie hurts," right?

Child:

Yeah.

Parent:

Also—and this is super important—if anyone *ever* tries to touch your penis (or vagina) or wants *you* to touch *theirs*, I want you to tell them no and tell me about it. Right away.

It's your body, and when you're a child, no one has the right to touch it. No one.

Child:
Even if it's someone I know?
Parent:
Yes. Even if it's someone you know. Friends. Teachers. Even family.

Even if they're nice. Even if they say it's a game. Even if they say not to tell.

And if that ever happens, I want you to say:

"No. I have to ask my mom (or dad or caregiver) first."
Child:
What if they say not to tell?
Parent:
Then you come tell me even faster. They are lying.

You will never get in trouble for telling me the truth. Ever.

If someone breaks that rule, that's on them—not you. You did nothing wrong. Even if you are too scared to say no. But Mommy might need to call the police because that's how serious this rule is.

Remember: If someone breaks the body safety rule, it's never your fault. It's theirs. And the police and Mommy will be mad at them, not you.

safe vs. unsafe touch—no exceptions

. . .

NO EXCEPTIONS
One of the most important safety rules you can teach your child is the difference between safe and unsafe touch.

What Is Safe Touch?
Safe touch is:

- A hug from someone you love *when you want it*
- Holding hands to cross the street
- Getting help from a parent with a bath or at the doctor's office *with permission*
- Putting on sunscreen with a trusted adult you know

Safe touch is about care, comfort, and your permission. You get to say yes or no. And you can change your mind.

How to explain permission: "Permission means you *ask* before you touch someone or something, and they have to say it's okay. Like if you want to borrow a toy—you don't just take it, right? You ask first. Same with hugs or touching. You always ask, and you can say no, too. Your body is yours."

● What Is Unsafe Touch?
Unsafe touch is:

- Any touch to the parts of your body covered by a swimsuit (your privates)
- Any touch that makes you feel weird, scared, confused, or uncomfortable—even if the person says it's a secret or a game
- Being asked to touch someone else's private parts
- Being shown private parts, photos, or videos that feel wrong

Unsafe touch might not always hurt—but it always breaks the body safety rules. And if it breaks the rule, you tell someone. Right away.

🚫 No Exceptions Means No Exceptions

This is where it has to be black and white. Kids need to hear this clearly:

"No one is allowed to touch your private parts or ask you to touch theirs. Not a friend. Not a cousin. Not a grown-up. Not even someone you trust or someone who says it's a game or a secret. The only people who can help with private parts are the people taking care of you—like Mommy, Daddy, Grandma, or your doctor—and only if a parent says it's okay and is there with you. No exceptions. Ever."

🚫 No Secrets About Bodies. Period.

One of the first things predators teach a child is to keep it a secret.

That's why your child needs to hear this rule loud and clear:

"We never keep secrets about our bodies."

Not for anyone. Not ever.

▶ Why This Matters

Abusers often say things like:

- "This is our special secret."
- "Don't tell anyone, or we'll both get in trouble."
- "If you tell, no one will believe you."
- "This is just between us."
- "Your mom will be really mad if you tell."
- "You don't want to make her sad, do you? Be a good kid."

They use secrecy to trap kids in silence—and that silence gives them power.

But when your child knows that secrets about bodies are never allowed and that it's not their fault no matter what, they're more likely to speak up—even if they're scared or confused.

They need to know:

- You won't be mad.
- They won't be in trouble.
- And if someone says otherwise, that person is lying.

You are taking away the predator's strongest weapon: silence.

We'll talk about how to practice this rule with your child in the next section.

💬 What to Say to Your Child:

"We don't keep secrets about our bodies. If someone ever touches you in a way that makes you feel weird or says something about your penis or vagina—and tells you not to tell—you come tell me right away.

Even if they say it's a secret or a game or if they try to scare you.

You will never be in trouble for telling me the truth. Never.

And if someone says you will? They're lying."

✅ Teach This Rule Early—and Repeat Often

Use real-life examples to help it stick:

- "If someone gives you a gift and says not to tell me—that's not okay. We don't keep secrets from Mom or Dad."
- "If someone tells you a secret that makes you feel yucky or nervous, that's a sign you should tell me right away."

And help them understand the difference between a surprise and a secret:

"A surprise is something we keep quiet *for a little while*—like a birthday present.

But a secret about your body? That's never okay."

"your body, your rules"— they don't owe affection to anyone

• • •

"YOUR BODY, YOUR RULES"—THEY Don't Owe Affection to Anyone

One of the easiest ways to teach body autonomy to kids is by letting them choose when and how to show affection.

That means they never have to:

- Hug Grandma if they don't want to
- Sit on Uncle's lap if it makes them uncomfortable
- Say yes to a kiss or a cuddle just to be "polite"

This isn't about rudeness—it's about safety.

Kids need to know:

"You're allowed to say no. Even to grown-ups. Even to people you love. Your body is yours, and you never owe anyone a hug, a kiss, or a snuggle."

When we force physical affection, even with good intentions, we teach kids that their comfort doesn't matter. Worse, we teach them to ignore their instincts.

Let them say no. Celebrate their boundaries. That's how we raise kids who speak up when something feels wrong.

the "no game" (how to practice saying no)
. . .

🍫 **THE POWER OF "NO"** and Walking Away

Kids are often taught to be polite, quiet, and cooperative—but when it comes to their bodies, we need to teach them the exact opposite.

If something feels wrong, they have the right to say "NO" —loudly—and get away.

That means:
- Saying "NO, I don't like that!"
- Getting up and walking away
- Telling a safe adult right away

We have to make it very clear that they are *never* being rude for protecting themselves. In fact, we need to celebrate it.

Practice saying it together:
"NO! I don't like that!"
"STOP! I'm telling my mom!"
"I don't keep secrets. I'm going to tell."

Let them use their voice. Let them rehearse being loud,

firm, and clear. These moments might feel silly now, but one day, that voice might save them.

The "NO Game" (How to Practice Saying No)

Purpose:

To help your child feel confident using their voice, setting boundaries, and recognizing when to walk away.

What You Say to Your Child:

"We're going to play a game in which you get to say NO really loud and strong! If someone ever does something that makes you feel weird, scared, or uncomfortable, you have the right to say NO and get away. Ready?"

How to Play:

1 Set the tone

Say, "This is just a practice game. I'm going to pretend to ask you to do something silly or something you don't like. You get to say NO in a strong voice, okay?"

2 Act it out with playful, pretend examples:
- "Can I tickle you even if you don't want me to?"
- "Can I touch your vagina (or penis)?"
- "Can you keep this a secret from your mom?"
- "It's just a game—can I show you something fun about my pee-pee?"

3 Your child yells "NO!" or "STOP!"

Cheer them on! Clap, high-five, and say, "That was awesome! You used your voice! You protected your body!"

4 Practice walking away

Have them say "NO!" and then take two big steps back.

Optional: Have them practice running to a safe adult (you, a teacher, etc.) and saying, "I need help."

code words, exit strategies, and the "what if" game

• • •

TEACHING your child how to *get out of uncomfortable or unsafe situations* is just as important as teaching them what's wrong.

🔑 Code Words

A code word is a secret word your child can use to let you know they need help, want to leave, or don't feel safe—without anyone else knowing what they mean.

"If you ever feel uncomfortable at someone's house or a party, you can call or text me and say the code word—like 'I miss our dog' or 'I left my teddy.' That means I'll come get you right away."

Make sure they know that if they use the code word, they won't get in trouble.

🚪 Exit Strategies

Teach your child that it's *always okay to leave* a situation that feels wrong. Give them permission to:
- Say they need to use the bathroom

- Ask to call home
- Go find a safe adult (a teacher or another parent)

Practice lines like:

"I don't feel good."

"I need to call my mom."

"I forgot I have to go home."

the "what if" game
. . .

🎲 THE "WHAT IF" Game

This game helps kids think through tricky situations ahead of time so they aren't caught off guard.

Ask questions like:
- "What if someone tells you to keep a secret about your body?"
- "What if your friend's older brother wants you to go somewhere alone with him?"
- "What if someone says they'll get you in trouble if you tell me something?"

Let your child come up with answers—then gently guide them if needed.

This kind of practice gives kids confidence, clarity, and power.

section 3: the places we overlook (and how to fix it)

. . .

"IT COULD NEVER HAPPEN to My Kid"—Yes, It Could.
One in four girls. One in six boys. That's the reality.

Every parent wants to believe their child is safe. It's comforting to think, *'That happens to other people's kids, not mine.'* But that mindset is exactly what predators count on. They count on our trusting nature. On our belief in the good of others. On us giving people the benefit of the doubt.

The truth is, predators don't look like monsters. They look like coaches, babysitters, favorite uncles, pastors, teachers—or even other kids. I've sat across from them in my office. I've worked with families who were shattered because they thought they were doing everything right—until they realized their blind spots. I've also sat across from a funny, charming, straight-A teenager who had sexually assaulted a kindergartener.

▶ Believing our children are untouchable doesn't protect them. It makes them more vulnerable.

We parents have to accept that abuse doesn't happen only *"out there."* It happens in good families and safe neighborhoods, too. Awareness is our first line of defense.

Here's the most important truth of all:

▶ *<u>Secrecy is a predator's strongest weapon. If we talk about safety and abuse openly and often, we take that power away. If your child knows how to talk about their body, how to report something that feels wrong, and that they'll be believed—you've just made your child a far more difficult target.</u>*

▶ Why Early Conversations Work: A Personal Example

I was 11 years old the first time someone tried to sexually manipulate me.

I spent a lot of time outside with the neighborhood kids. Some of them had older friends who also hung around. One day, after most of the kids had gone home for lunch, I was still outside. A teenage boy—about 17—named Stefan sat behind a fence and started asking me sexual questions. He asked if I had ever seen people "do it" in movies. I told him I had seen adults kiss or women sit on men's laps at festivals.

Then, he told me to show him. He pointed to his lap and told me to sit on him.

In that moment, I froze. He was older. And the cool kid. I didn't know if I was supposed to do what he said. But something stopped me: my mom's voice.

She had always asked me directly if anyone had ever touched me inappropriately. She didn't make it scary—just clear. I had always said no because nothing had happened. But she made sure I understood that if someone *did* try to touch me, it would be wrong, and I should come to her.

That messaging helped me decide what to do.

So I told him no. He tried to pressure me—"*Oh, come on. It's nothing bad.*" But I turned and walked away. Fast. I still remember the moment I left.

That one repeated message from my mom made the difference. That's why these conversations matter. Not once. Not when they're older. Regularly and early.

overtrusting people you think are safe

· · ·

THIS ONE IS HARD. It might hurt. We don't want to believe someone we love—or someone our kids love—could hurt them.

But 90% of children who are abused are abused by someone they know and trust.

Here's what that means: You might feel totally comfortable leaving your kid with a family friend, a cousin, a neighbor who's "great with kids," or even that uncle. But predators often *earn your trust first*. That's their playbook.

This doesn't mean you need to panic or live in fear. It means you need boundaries, supervision, and honest conversations with your kids—even about people you trust.

▶ Their biggest weapon is secrecy. Convincing the victim that silence is safest. That no one will believe them. That it's their fault. Let's take that power away and add a few more guards.

Ask yourself:

- Does this adult seek one-on-one time with my child, especially in private spaces?

- Do they give my child gifts or seem to play favorites?
- Do they respect boundaries—*including my child's*?

You don't have to be paranoid, but you do have to be aware. Trust is earned. Supervision is non-negotiable.

sleepovers—how to rethink them

. . .

LET'S talk about the big one: sleepovers.

They can be fun. They can be harmless. But they're also one of the riskiest situations for child sexual abuse.

Your child has a one in four chance of being sexually abused. Sleepovers often mean hours of unsupervised time in someone else's home—with people you might not know well. There could be visitors. Older kids.

Who are they?

My children won't attend sleepovers. Period. They can have them at our house, where I know exactly who's around and what's happening, but I will not hand them over for the night.

As a therapist, I can't un-hear the countless stories of abuse that happened during a sleepover at a "friend's" house. That reality has branded itself into my mind. I won't gamble with my children's safety for the sake of fitting in or sparing someone's feelings.

Your child won't suffer lifelong trauma because they weren't allowed to go on sleepovers. But a sexual assault can leave scars for life.

If you still choose to allow them:

- Make sure your child is already comfortable discussing their body and boundaries with you.
- Make sure they know: no secrets. Ever. And they can always come to you.
- Teach them to say, "This is wrong. I'm telling my mom. Or the police." That kind of directness scares predators.
- Allow sleepovers only with families you know deeply and trust completely.
- No exceptions. No guests staying over that night. No unplanned visitors.
- Teach your child to stick with friends they know and to avoid being alone with unfamiliar kids or adults.
- Set clear rules: open doors, no changing clothes in front of others, and no secrets. No sleeping in rooms alone. Girls with girls. Boys with boys.
- Give them an exit strategy like a secret code word to text or to say if they want out.

The same goes for playdates and one-on-one time. You don't need to hover like a helicopter, but you *do* need to be a present, observant parent. Ask questions. Show up early. Pay attention.

one-on-one time—like tutoring or lessons

. . .

IT'S NOT JUST SLEEPOVERS. One-on-one settings like music lessons, tutoring, or private coaching also give an adult uninterrupted access to your child.

These environments can be positive and helpful—but they also require additional supervision.

Here's what you can do:

• Ask if you can record the session. Many professionals are used to this and will agree without hesitation. You can always say something like:

"I'm just recording the lesson so we can listen back at home and practice together. Do you mind?"

• Stay close. Sit just outside the door—or inside the room.

• Drop in unannounced occasionally, even after you feel comfortable. Let the adult know you're engaged and aware.

If the teacher, coach, or tutor gets defensive about your presence or the idea of recording, that's a red flag.

You are not being overbearing. You're parenting. Predators are far less likely to target a child whose parent is clearly involved and paying attention.

tech is a gateway
...

TECH IS A GATEWAY: Predators Don't Need to Be in the Room Anymore

Here's the terrifying truth: Your child's abuser might not even be in the same country.

Online grooming is real. It happens on games, messaging apps, social media, school forums—anywhere kids gather online.

Predators know how to blend in. They pretend to be peers. They flatter. They build trust. Then, they escalate.

This is why no child should be online without regular check-ins and clear boundaries.

What to do:

• No access, no tech. If your child wants access, you must also have access.

• Know every app they use.

• Keep all accounts private.

• Teach them what is and isn't okay to share (names, photos, school, location).

• Show them how to report or block people.

• Let them know they can always come to you—no matter what.

Grooming can start young. The earlier you talk, the safer they are.

Again, secrecy is the predator's power. Talking regularly, openly, and without shame takes that power away.

what you can do differently today

• • •

HERE'S THE GOOD NEWS: You can make changes now that build a safer future for your kids. Start with these:

- **Have the talk.** Not once. Not in vague terms. Often. Be specific. Use correct body part names. Practice saying no. Practice what to do if someone crosses a line. Check in often: *"Has anyone ever tried to touch your penis or vagina?"* Normalize asking and answering without shame.
- **Set boundaries.** Don't force hugs or kisses. Don't laugh off "teasing" that makes your child uncomfortable. Show them: *Your body belongs to you.*
- **Build your exit plans.** Come up with code words or text phrases they can use if they want to leave a situation. Practice how they'd use these words or phrases.
- **Supervise actively.** Don't assume someone is safe just because they're family or friendly. **Trust your gut—and your child's.**
- **Open the door on tech.** Make it normal to talk about what's happening online. Your child should *know* they can come to you with anything—and you won't freak out or punish them. You'll listen.

section 4: safety drills and real-life conversations

. . .

THIS TALK DOESN'T HAVE to Be Scary—It Has to Be Clear

Let's get one thing straight: Talking about sexual abuse doesn't have to be scary. But it *does* have to be honest, clear, and direct.

Your child is already learning about danger in other areas. We teach our children not to touch hot stoves. We explain why they wear seatbelts. Schools run fire drills and tornado drills.

Talking about body safety should be just as normal.

You are not traumatizing your child by having these conversations. You're protecting them.

The real danger isn't the conversation—it's the silence.

secrecy is their biggest weapon

. . .

SECRECY IS Their Biggest Weapon—Break the Silence First

I've said it before, and I'll say it again: Secrecy is the predator's biggest weapon.

They rely on silence. They groom children to stay quiet. To feel confused. To think no one will believe them. That they did something wrong. That it's their fault.

You destroy that weapon by talking about abuse openly, early, and often.

Tell your child that there are people in the world who hurt kids. Tell them clearly:

No one is allowed to touch your penis, butt, or vagina.

If someone tries, your child can and *should* tell you.

They can say NO.

They can walk away.

And they will never get in trouble for telling you.

This doesn't scare children—it empowers them.

how to practice situations like fire drills
• • •

JUST LIKE WE practice exiting a building in a fire, we need to practice handling unsafe or confusing situations. Repetition builds confidence.

Here are simple, real-life safety drills to run with your child. You can do them in the car, during dinner, at bedtime—anywhere.

◆ How to Practice Situations Like Fire Drills

Just like we practice exiting a building in a fire, we need to practice handling unsafe or confusing situations. Repetition builds confidence.

Here are simple, real-life safety drills to run with your child. You can do them in the car, during dinner, at bedtime—anywhere.

◆ "What if a grown-up wants you to keep a secret?"

Teach your child the difference between *secrets* and *surprises*. Surprises are short-term and fun—like birthday gifts.

45

Secrets are meant to be hidden—and that's dangerous.
What to say:

- "If any adult tells you to keep a secret from me, that's a red flag. You should always tell me."
- "If someone says, 'This is our little secret,' I want you to come tell me right away—even if they say I'll get mad."

Practice response:
"No, I don't keep secrets from my mom/dad. I'm going to tell them."

◆ "What if someone makes you uncomfortable?"
Abuse doesn't always start with something obvious. Often, it starts with small actions that feel "off." Teach your child to trust their gut.
What to say:

- "If someone makes you feel weird, or makes your stomach feel funny, or does something that just doesn't feel right—even if they didn't touch you—you can come tell me."
- "Even if they're a grown-up. Even if you like them."

Practice response:
"That makes me uncomfortable. I'm going to leave now."

◆ "What if your friend says something happened to them?"
Kids need to know what to do if a friend tells them about abuse. Most won't know how to handle it unless we show them.

What to say:

- "If a friend tells you someone touched them or hurt them, you have to tell me. That's not tattling—it's helping."
- "You don't have to fix it. Just come get me or another trusted adult, and we'll help them together."

Practice response:
"That sounds scary. I think we need to tell an adult."

repetition builds confidence

. . .

REPETITION BUILDS CONFIDENCE

This is not a one-time talk. These conversations should happen regularly, just like brushing teeth or practicing reading.

Short, clear, and consistent is what makes it stick.

Tips:

- Use car rides or bedtime for quick check-ins—especially before/after your child starts a new school, camp, or activity.
- Make it a normal part of life—not a dramatic "serious talk" every time.
- Praise your child when they set boundaries or speak up, even in small situations.
- Stay calm. Your tone matters. You want them to know you're always a safe place.

create a shame-free zone
. . .

YOUR HOME SHOULD BE a place where there's no shame in talking about bodies, boundaries, or anything uncomfortable.

If your child feels embarrassed or afraid to bring something up, they'll stay quiet—and predators rely on that silence.

What helps:

• Use proper names for body parts. This removes confusion and shame.

• Don't overreact if your child brings something up. Stay calm and curious.

• Remind them often:

"You can always tell me anything. I will always listen. I will always help you. You did nothing wrong."

section 5: if something happens—what now?
. . .

FIRST—NEVER Forget This

If your child has been abused, or if you even suspect it, you must remember one thing:

This is not your fault. This is not your child's fault.

You and your child have become the targets of a predator. A manipulator. A monster who knew exactly how to gain trust, cross boundaries, and cause harm.

The blame lies 100% with the person who chose to abuse.

No parenting mistake, no missed sign, no decision you made gives someone the right to hurt your child. And your child—whether they froze, complied, didn't speak up, or waited to tell—did nothing wrong.

Read that again if you need to.

signs of abuse most parents miss

. . .

NOT EVERY CHILD will tell you when something happens. Some don't have the words. Others stay silent out of fear, shame, or pressure from the abuser.

Here are signs parents often overlook:

- Sudden fear of a specific person, place, or activity (especially ones they previously enjoyed)
- Sexualized behavior or language that's not age-appropriate
- Acting out sexually with toys or other children
- Frequent nightmares, bedwetting, or trouble sleeping
- Unexplained anger, aggression, or withdrawal
- Stomachaches, headaches, or other physical symptoms without a clear cause
- Extreme clinginess or regression in behavior (thumb-sucking, baby talk, accidents)
- Going quiet or being withdrawn after visiting a certain person
- Reluctance to be alone with someone they used to trust

No single sign proves abuse—but when patterns emerge, pay attention. Don't brush it off.

if your child discloses— what to say, what not to say

• • •

IF YOUR CHILD tells you something happened, how you respond will shape their healing.

What to do:
- Stay calm, even if you're panicking inside.
- Believe them. Say, "Thank you for telling me. *I believe you.*"
- Reassure them: *"You did nothing wrong. This is not your fault."*
- Tell them you will protect them moving forward.

What not to say:
- "Are you sure?" or "That doesn't sound like them."
  → This feels like doubt and can make your child shut down.
- "Why didn't you tell me sooner?"
  → This adds shame and guilt to an already overwhelming experience.
- "Don't tell anyone."
  → This reinforces secrecy, which abusers count on.

Instead, say:
"I'm so glad you told me."

"You did the right thing."
"I'm going to help keep you safe."
"This is not your fault. It's never your fault."

when you suspect something but don't have proof

. . .

IF YOU'RE unsure but your instincts are telling you something is off, do not ignore it.

What to do:

1 Document what you observe. Behaviors, dates, conversations—anything that feels off.

2 Create safety. Limit or stop one-on-one contact with the person in question.

3 Ask open-ended questions over time, not in a pressuring or interrogative way.

4 Trust your gut. You don't need proof to act on a concern.

who to call, how to report, and where to find support
• • •

YOU DON'T NEED to confirm abuse to report it. That's not your role. Your job is to raise the flag so professionals can step in.

Who to contact:

• Child abuse hotline in your state (can remain anonymous)
• Child protective services (CPS) in your local area
• 911 if your child is in immediate danger
• Your child's pediatrician (they are mandated reporters)
• The school if the suspected abuser is a teacher, staff member, or student

get professional help right away

. . .

WHETHER THERE'S BEEN A DISCLOSURE, a strong suspicion, or even just a confusing encounter, seek therapeutic support for your child. Don't wait.

Why it matters:

• A trained therapist can help your child process the experience in a safe, age-appropriate way.

• Therapy helps prevent long-term emotional or psychological damage—even if abuse is only suspected.

• Support for *you* as a parent is just as important. You'll need guidance on what to say, how to respond, and how to handle the aftermath.

Where to start:

• Your pediatrician can refer you to a child trauma therapist in your area.

• The National Child Traumatic Stress Network (www.nctsn.org) offers a directory of trauma-informed providers.

• RAINN (www.rainn.org) provides a 24/7 confidential hotline (1-800-656-HOPE) and connects families with local resources.

- Darkness to Light (www.d2l.org) offers prevention and response tools, plus links to therapeutic services.
- Stop It Now (www.stopitnow.org) provides confidential helplines and action steps for concerned adults.
- Child advocacy centers often offer free or low-cost therapy and case coordination. Search "child advocacy center near me" or visit www.nationalcac.org.

Make sure the therapist is trained in child sexual abuse and trauma. Look for approaches like play therapy, TF-CBT (trauma-focused cognitive behavioral therapy), or EMDR.

You don't have to do this alone—and your child should not have to process this alone.

final chapter: no more easy targets

. . .

WE DON'T HAVE to be perfect parents. We don't have to get every step right.

But we *do* have to act. Talk. Ask questions. Stay alert.

Trust our instincts.

Predators thrive in silence. They seek out children who don't know the rules. Who haven't been taught to speak up. Who've never had these conversations at home.

But you're already doing something powerful: You're paying attention.

Let's close this out with a clear, no-nonsense checklist.

your parent checklist

. . .

☑ **YOUR PARENT CHECKLIST:** What to Teach, What to Watch, What to Trust

What to Teach Your Child

- The correct names for their private parts (penis, vagina, butt, chest, breasts).
- That no one is allowed to touch them—or ask to be touched.
- That they can always say **NO**, even to an adult.
- The difference between surprises (okay) and secrets (not okay).
- That they can come to you no matter what—even if someone told them not to.
- That abuse is **never, ever their fault**.

What to Watch For

- Changes in behavior: anger, withdrawal, regression, or fear of specific people.
- Inappropriate sexual language or behavior for their age.
- Nightmares, anxiety, bedwetting, or unexplained physical complaints.

- Sudden secrecy, especially after visits with certain people.
- Avoidance of someone they previously trusted.

What to Trust
- **Your gut.** If something feels off, it probably is.
- **Your child's instincts.** If they say they're uncomfortable, believe them.
- **Your right to ask questions.** No one is above your child's safety.
- **Your ability to pivot.** If you missed something before, you can still take action now.
- **Your role.** You are your child's first and most powerful line of defense.

reminder: you won't do this perfectly—and that's okay

• • •

⚠ YOU WON'T DO This Perfectly—And That's Okay

You'll fumble a few of these conversations. You might wish you'd started earlier. You might have moments of doubt or discomfort.

That's okay.

What matters most is that you're trying. You're showing up. You're having the hard conversations.

And you're not staying silent.

Predators count on silence, avoidance, and discomfort.

You're already taking that away from them.

a few final words of encouragement
. . .

IF YOU'VE MADE it this far, it's because you care deeply about protecting your child—and that alone means a lot.

You're not just raising a child. You're raising someone who knows:
- Their body belongs to them.
- Their voice matters.
- They can speak up—and be believed.

You're not alone in this. You're part of a growing group of parents who are saying, "Not my child. Not anymore."

You're making your child harder to groom, harder to silence, and **harder to hurt**.

You've got this. And your child has you.

That's what makes all the difference.

before you close this book—please remember
. . .

📌 **IF ABUSE** has already happened, or if you're only just now discovering it:

🔹 **This is not your fault. And it's not your child's fault.** 🔹

You and your child were targeted by someone who knew exactly how to manipulate, lie, and take advantage of trust.

A predator. A person who made the choice to hurt.

🔹 **The blame belongs 100% to them.** 🔹

No parenting decision—no missed sign, no moment of trust, no benefit of the doubt—gives anyone the right to hurt your child.

And your child? Whether they froze, complied, didn't speak up, or waited to tell?

They did nothing wrong.

Read that again if you need to. And hold onto it. Because that truth is the foundation of healing—for both you and your child.

thank you!
...

DEAR READER,

Thank you for reading "Not My Kid." Please consider leaving a review on your preferred retailer's website (like Amazon, Goodreads, Barnes & Noble, etc.), and spread the word. Reviews and shares help spread the word, and the more people who read this guide, the more children we can save.

I don't make a single dime on this book. The mission is more important than anything else. I do, however, write fiction books—mostly thrillers and horror thrillers. You can check them out here:

Amazon Author profile:
https://www.amazon.com/stores/S.-T.-Ashman/author/B0BZPWPF6F
Newsletter: https://www.ashmanbooks.com
Instagram: https://www.instagram.com/booksbyashman/
TikTok: https://www.tiktok.com/@ashmanbooks
Join Ashman's Dark Thriller Facebook Group to Meet the Author:
https://www.facebook.com/profile.php?id=100094353614873

Contact: hello@ashmanbooks.com
Thank you for your support.
S. T. Ashman

about the author

S. T. Ashman is a writer who once delved into the criminal justice system as a psychotherapist. This role gifted her with a unique insight into the human psyche—both the beautiful and the deeply shadowed. She considers herself a crime-solving enthusiast, often daydreaming about being the female version of Columbo, solving mysteries while rocking a trench coat. Her writing audaciously defies norms and promises to keep readers engrossed in a nail-biting adventure.

When she's not busy crafting suspenseful tales, she's chasing after her nap-resistant kids, binge-watching TV with her husband, or … actually, that pretty much covers it.

She aims to bend your brain, tickle your intrigue, and leave you pondering long after the last page. Come join her on her journeys.

www.ingramcontent.com/pod-product-compliance
Lightning Source LLC
Chambersburg PA
CBHW020547080526
44583CB00013B/1042